I shall rise again

Dr. Aftab Ahmed

BlueRose ONE.com
Stories Matter
NewDelhi • London

BLUEROSE PUBLISHERS
U.K.

BlueRose ONE.com
Stories Matter
NewDelhi • London

For permissions requests or inquiries regarding this publication, please contact:

BLUEROSE PUBLISHERS
www.BlueRoseONE.com
info@bluerosepublishers.com
+4407342408967

ISBN: 978-93-6783-920-1

Cover design: Daksh
Typesetting: Tanya Raj Upadhyay

First Edition: January 2025

To my children,
Shiara, Yaseen and Farhan,
And to my young readers

Life is a journey filled with unexpected challenges, twists, and turns. Throughout this journey, you will face moments of joy and moments of despair, triumphs, and setbacks. Remember, it is not the challenges you face that define you, but how you respond to them.

This book is for you, a guide through the ups and downs of life. When faced with challenges, remember that each setback is a lesson, each failure a stepping stone. Never give up, no matter how tough the journey becomes. Rise, fight back, and let your resilience shine. You have the strength to overcome any obstacle and the courage to turn dreams into reality. May this book inspire you to persevere and find beauty in every struggle. You are my pride and joy, and I believe in your endless potential.

"There is a stubbornness about me that never can bear to be frightened at the will of others. My courage always rises at every attempt to intimidate me."

Jane Austen, Pride and Prejudice

ACKNOWLEDGEMENTS

I owe my deepest gratitude to my parents for their unwavering trust and belief in me. To my wife, who has stood by my side with great support and love, thank you. To my children, whose joy and strength inspire me every day, I am forever grateful. And to my loyal friends, who never once doubted my potential, your faith has been a cornerstone of this journey. This book is a testament to the incredible people in my life.

But one person who had a tremendous impact on me in becoming who I am today is my father.

"If I pass through a struggle, you are my strength.

If I doubt myself, I see your faith.

If I see my success, I feel your pride.

And if I am living a dream, you are my lifeline.

I wish I can be to my children what you are to me as my father."

This book is dedicated to every father's unflinching support, motivation, and love towards their children.

TABLE OF CONTENTS

DESTINIES BLESSED

No matter the height of the boundless sky,
No matter the times I dare to fly,
No matter if I fall and cry,
No matter how often I fail and sigh,

My hopes shall never wither or die,
My heart won't ever cease to try,

Survival is not my sole quest,
I'm here to surpass every test,
To those who doubt and jest,
Watch me rise as destinies blessed!

TRANSFORMATION

Sometimes growth is slow, imperceptible,
Unseen like whispers in the wind, intangible.

In the mirror's gaze, you find no trace,
Yet within, transformation takes its place.

Layer by layer, a new self-unfurls,
Silently rewriting life's intricate swirls.

When adversity knocks, you rise anew,
Like a canvas of strength, painted beautifully by you.

For what you become, my dear friend, is the key,
A reflection of faith, the promise of possibility.

LOOK INSIDE

I stood in the dark of the night,
Not knowing what was wrong and what was right.

I had lost all hope, engulfed by despair,
In a grief so immense, it would not spare.

And then, I saw a light that shone brightly,
A hope that rekindled my resolve to fight keenly.

It wasn't from anywhere far apart,
It came right from the window of my heart.

All the darkness we see outside,
Can be vanquished if we believe in the light inside.

BELIEVE IN YOUR ESSENCE

In the eyes of the world, you may be judged,
But don't let their opinion define your path,
Your essence remains hidden from their view,
Revealed only by the mirror of your own heart.

WHISPERS OF THE HEART

In the silence of your solitude,
Listen to the whispers of your heart,
For what the mind seeks in its thoughts,
The heart already knows.

DAY AND NIGHT

Beneath the night's celestial glow, stars dance and gleam,
Should I surrender to slumber, chasing a splendid dream?

Or with morning's arrival, as the sun greets with golden beams,
Should I chart my path, to bring my dreams to life's stream?

As dusk and dawn exchange their roles in ceaseless flight,
Our dreams will stay as mere dreams unless we strive with all our might.

BE YOUR KIND OF BEAUTIFUL

Beauty can manifest in any attire,
It can be pristine and perfect,
It can be ragged and wrecked,
It's not in what you see but how you decipher.

THE NEW BEGINNINGS

You are not what you have lost,
You are what you have loved,
Embrace the loss,
But believe in the promise of new beginnings.

WILD FLOWER

I am not a flower destined to wither,
I am not the one who scurries hither and thither,
I will survive, bloom, and thrive in any season,
I will stand tall and always fight for my reason.

ECHOES OF KINDNESS

In the quiet chambers of the heart, where compassion
blooms and love take part,

The world mirrors what you give it,
A dance of reciprocity, every bit by bit.

If you sow happiness from your soul,
The universe echoes the joy in whole,

If you let the peace unfurl its wings,
The tranquility blossoms in all surrounding things,

If you allow the love to weave a cosmic thread,
It connects the hearts across expanse that is vast
spread.

Give freely and watch them multiply,
Like a constellation of stars lighting up the dark sky.

A BEAUTIFUL MIND

When beauty graces your thoughts,
When serenity resides in your hearts,
The world around you becomes cheerful,
And every moment turns blissful.

ADAMANTINE

In a sky that you ache to explore,
In a race that keeps you moving,
In a sea that you dare to plunge,
In a battle that you wield a sword,
In a wound that you struggle with pain,
In a heart that holds your myriad emotions,
In a mind that conflicts with your reason,

When you persevere, my dear,
I believe, a day will come,

When you fly without falling,
When you speed without crashing,
When you swim without drowning,
When you fight without quitting,
When you smile without grieving,
When you love without doubting,
When you think without worrying,

That day would be the day,
When you realize the true Zen of living.

BEAUTIFUL IMPERFECTIONS

There is a beauty in brokenness,
There is a blessing in Ignorance,
There is a healing in solitude,
There is a power in silence,
There is a resilience in pain,
There is an opportunity in darkness,
There is an order in all the chaos,
All the things in life may not be perfect,
Yet there is a charm and wisdom in the imperfect symphony of life.

OPEN YOUR SOUL

There are mysteries that abound the vast unexplored sky,
There is more to life than that which meets the naked eye,
When the window to your soul begins to open,
You will see and feel the most amazing things happen.

THE LIGHT WE CANNOT SEE

There is darkness in the world,
The pain that breaks you,
The suffering that engulfs you,
The sorrow that destroys you,

Yet,
There is a light that brightens the world,
A hope that strengthens you,
A resilience that shapes you,
A happiness that cheers you,

All the darkness in the world cannot make this light disappear,
It's not the light outside, it's the light within,
It is the light that we cannot see,
And it is what makes our life worth living.

I BEGAN TO RISE

For long,
I fell prey to the comfort of a placid life,
Not willing to rise and risk again,
The fear of failure freezing my flight,

And then,
I burst the bubble of my mundane life,
I began to rise again,
And challenged myself to an unknown height,

My dear,
I embraced the story of my life,
And so, I began to rise again,
Determined not to give up without a fight

LIVE IT ALL

Each one of us boards the train of our life;
But none of us really knows where it stops.
The best we can do is to enjoy the journey,
Meet the people who board at different stations,
Make memories out of those encounters,
Let go of those whose journey is over,
And relish the time spent with loved ones,
Without bothering about the final destination,
Because it's the moments that matter, and not where they end.
When you reach the end, you should be able to say,
"My dear, I lived it all!"

THE PATH

On a stormy night,
On a lonely path,
I ventured with uncertainty in my heart,
I braved the fear that stroked my mind,
Would I succeed in my journey?

I tripped and fell in despair,
Hit by harsh winds, drenched in cold,
Yet I pulled myself up,
Clung to the plank of hope,
And moved forward with tireless energy,

I realized I got it wrong,
It was not about the destination,
But about the way to self-discovery,
Not how fast I can go,
But how far I can make it.

My dear, so set forth on your journey,
Embrace the lessons along the way, it matters not whether you reach the end,
For all journeys need not be successful.
Yet, a path to enlightenment is never a failure.

LIMITLESS

In the journey to summit, my dear friend,
When you reach the zenith, you think it's the end,

But then you realize, where the peak ends, starts the sky,
And you spread your wings, ready to fly.

As you soar above the clouds to transcend,
You'll find the courage on which you can depend,

For every limit is a beginning in disguise,
And every goodbye, a hello to new skies.

SURVIVE AND FIGHT

Success always kissed my feet,
I had never faced a failure,
I was unfamiliar with the taste of loss,

I would always be prepared,
Putting forth my best efforts,
I believed it was a simple recipe for success,

And then failure struck me with a jolt of surprise,
I faltered despite my best efforts,
How could I? What went wrong?

I searched within myself for a reason,
I found none to behold,
I hadn't lost, they simply denied me victory,

Life's battles aren't always fair,
It's not always about winning,
Sometimes, survival alone would suffice,

There is glory in success after failure,
Yet greater still is in rising from unjust defeat,
And emerging in time towards ultimate triumph,

Sometimes, failure isn't truly failure
And success isn't absolute success,
What defines you is your unwavering will to endure
and fight.

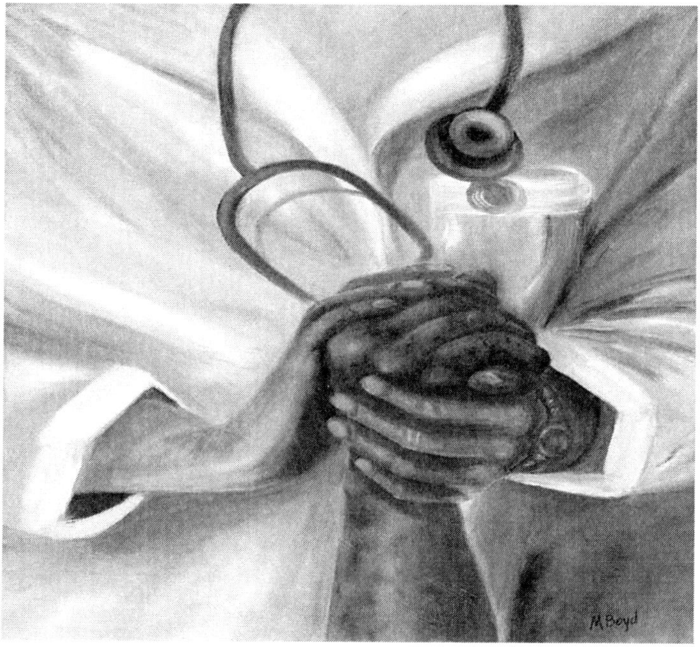
M Boyd

WHITE COAT ANGELS

I witnessed that smile of gratitude,
It's all that matters where we work,
Where life teeters on the edge,
And hope blooms anew with each heartbeat,

I also saw a face etched in deep sorrow,
A life slipping away despite our best,
We carry the weight of these loses,
A silent ache, that lingers in our soul,

Before I could dwell on this fragility of life,
I get a call from ER,
There is a new life hanging in delicate balance,
I get ready to fight again for another battle of life,

For we are the guardians of hope,
The unsung heroes in white coats,
Fighting unseen battles with heart aflame,
In the theatre of life, we rise again, and again!

BRING IT OUT

Let the story within you come out in your writings,
Let the rhythm in your heart spread out as your music,
Let the picture inside your mind manifest in your art,
Let the emotions in you find their true connect,
Let the life in you resurrect with smile again,
For only when you let out, you let in the new beginnings.

AWAKE

It's the same sky that holds stars and the moon for you and me,
Yet, the world imprisons us within the boundaries we cannot free,
Why look for the glow in the dark night?
When you can be the candle that brings light,
So, build bridges, and let the barriers break,
It always begins with ONE to get awake.

EARTH AND HEAVEN

We live on Earth and think about heaven,
A heaven where everything is picture-perfect,
A heaven where you experience no pain,
A heaven where there is no sorrow,
A heaven where you face no challenges,
A heaven where you don't need to strive,
A heaven where you do not age,
A heaven where you do not die,
A heaven where everything is bountiful.

And so, I ponder, what does Earth offer?
A life which is not perfect but real,
A journey that inflicts pain but also makes you stronger,
A rainbow of emotions laced with love, joy, and sorrow,
An opportunity to face obstacles and overcome them,
A body that grows old, but gracefully,
A place where there is enough to survive with happiness.

Yet,
We look forward to the wishful heaven,
And close our eyes to the reality of the present,
A perfect life in heaven is a wonderful dream,

But an imperfect life on Earth can also be beautiful,
For there is charm in the chaos of our life,
We face hell and heaven both on Earth,
While we journey from this ephemeral world to the eternal realm.

THE POWER OF YOU

You learn,
You act,
You survive!

You try,
You fail,
You rise.

You love,
You lose,
You heal.

You live,
You strive,
You die.

Between what you are,
And what you become,
What makes or breaks you,
is only—You!

PHOENIX

The world may fall apart,
You may lose everything you built,
But even in that abyss, it is not the end,
If you believe, you can build something new,
And make your world whole again,
A phoenix never gives up.

THE LIGHT OF LOVE

In this near dystopic world,
There is a dearth of love,
A dearth of recognition,
A dearth of eyes seeking the vulnerable,
A dearth of empathy for the broken.

But here is a thing,
When you light the lamp of love,
And when you care to love freely,
You never know how many souls it will touch,
And how far its rays will travel,

For love is an alchemy that transforms lives,
It transcends all the barriers,
And its light never ever dies.

TAKE THAT STEP

Every step that you take,
Every storm that you sail,
Every odd that you beat,
You redefine yourself, time and again,
And
When you reach the end of your journey,
You are not the same who started it,
You become,
You become what you believed in,
The best version of yourself.
Take that step!

OWN

Own what you see and think,

If you see from others eyes, you will always be in their prison,

And if you think as others think, you will always be caged,

Only by being YOU, you can set yourself free.

HERE I COME

Here I come,
Breaking the shackles that pinned me down,

Here I come,
Overcoming the fear that gripped my heart,

Here I come,
Trusting my instincts beyond everything else,

Here I come,
Rising from the ashes of my failure,

Here I come,
Striving to ignite the flame of hope,

Here I come,
Believing in the spirit of my indomitable will.

WHEN I AM GONE

When I am gone, as we all must go,
In the vast expanse of time and space, will I be lost forever?

If you remember me,
It means a part of what I was to you still lingers.

Even though we may be far apart,
You can still summon me with ease.

Though I no longer exist,
You can still picture my visage in your mind.

In the midst of silence,
You can still hear my words in your heart.

Even in solitude,
You can still feel my comforting presence.

When I die, I will still live on,
For as long as you remember me, I will forever be alive.

BOOKS BY SAME AUTHOR

Rehan
Love is like a rainbow
Embracing life
Sunshine and dewdrops

Available on *Notion press, Amazon, and Flipkart*

Rehan is a beautiful tale of love, longing, ambition and friendship.

Rehan is a typical lad whose world revolves around cricket and friends. He is also extremely attached to his grandmother, who is a great pillar of support and strength. Just when everything seems to be going well, his whole world comes crashing one day, resulting in Rehan giving up what he loves a lot. Thereafter, life takes on a whole new meaning for Rehan.

Love is like a Rainbow is a touching anthology on love. If life is a mix of sunny and stormy days, love makes it beautiful with its different shades.

Love is often contextual. It means different things to different people. It expresses its varied hue through perception from different hearts and minds. Love cannot be in one colour, it's a spectrum.

Experience this poetic journey, as the flame of love passes through many hearts to emanate its magnificent colours.

Embracing Life is a captivating and thought-provoking book of poems that delves into the dynamic and unpredictable nature of life. It is a collection of beautiful poems that explore the various challenges, highs and lows, joys and sorrows, and changing emotions that make up the fabric of our existence. It serves as a guiding light, encouraging readers to embrace every aspect of life and live it to the fullest.

Sunshine and Dewdrops is a captivating book that combines the beauty of images with the eloquence of verses and quotes. Each image in the book is carefully paired with words that encapsulate its story, creating a harmonious blend of visual and literary art. The book serves as a testament to the power of hope and the refreshing spirit of life.

ABOUT THE BOOK

This book, "I Shall Rise Again," is a testament to the unwavering spirit.

Within its pages, you'll discover verses that dance with hope, Stanzas that sing of courage, and lines that echo the heartbeat of fighters. Each poem, a beacon in the tempest, urging us to stand tall. To fight, not with swords or shields, but with the fire within. For we are more than mere mortals; we are warriors. Our scars tell stories of battles fought, victories won, and losses endured. And when the world conspires against us, we rise. We rise like the sun after a long, dark night. We rise like the phoenix from the ashes, reborn and unyielding. Our spirit, unbreakable; our resolve, unshakable. So let these verses be a balm for weary souls. May they remind you that even when the odds seem insurmountable, you possess the strength to defy fate. Embrace the journey of self-discovery, for imperfections are but brushstrokes on the canvas of resilience. And as you turn each page, may you find echoes of your own battles.

May you rise, again and again, against all odds. For within you lie the indomitable spirit that defies defeat.

ABOUT THE AUTHOR

Dr. Aftab Ahmed is one of the leading physicians in Hyderabad. He is currently a senior consultant physician and diabetologist at Apollo Hospital, Secunderabad. He graduated in medicine from Rangaraya Medical College and finished his post-graduate training at Andhra Medical College, Vishakapatnam. In his academic career, Dr. Ahmed has won several gold medals in various subjects.

Dr. Aftab is married to Reshma and has three children, Shiara, Yaseen and Farhan. He has a keen interest in literature and cricket and loves travelling. He has also authored four other books. His first book, *Rehan,* is a beautiful tale of love, ambition and friendship. *Love is like a rainbow,* his second book, is a touching anthology on love. *Embracing life,* his third book, is a collection of beautiful poems that explore the various challenges, highs and lows, joys and sorrows, and changing emotions that make up the fabric of our existence. *Sunshine and Dewdrops,* his last book release, is a captivating book that combines the beauty of images with the eloquence of verses and quotes

You can reach the author by emailing at.

draftab.books@yahoo.com